THIS IS ME!

RHYMING TREASURES

Edited By Roseanna Caswell

First published in Great Britain in 2022 by:

YoungWriters®
— Est. 1991 —

Young Writers
Remus House
Coltsfoot Drive
Peterborough
PE2 9BF
Telephone: 01733 890066
Website: www.youngwriters.co.uk

All Rights Reserved
Book Design by Ashley Janson
© Copyright Contributors 2021
Softback ISBN 978-1-80015-724-8

Printed and bound in the UK by BookPrintingUK
Website: www.bookprintinguk.com
YB0491K

FOREWORD

For Young Writers' latest competition This Is Me, we asked primary school pupils to look inside themselves, to think about what makes them unique, and then write a poem about it! They rose to the challenge magnificently and the result is this fantastic collection of poems in a variety of poetic styles.

Here at Young Writers our aim is to encourage creativity in children and to inspire a love of the written word, so it's great to get such an amazing response, with some absolutely fantastic poems. It's important for children to focus on and celebrate themselves and this competition allowed them to write freely and honestly, celebrating what makes them great, expressing their hopes and fears, or simply writing about their favourite things. This Is Me gave them the power of words. The result is a collection of inspirational and moving poems that also showcase their creativity and writing ability.

I'd like to congratulate all the young poets in this anthology, I hope this inspires them to continue with their creative writing.

CONTENTS

Aldbury CE Primary & Nursery School, Aldbury

Felix Cole (10)	1
Eric Niblock (11)	2
Rose Jenkins	4
Ben Woodhams	5
Amber Verinder (10)	6
Mitchell Phillips (10)	7
Maxwell MacGregor (9)	8
Leon Niblock (9)	9
Henrietta French (9)	10
Oliver Speck	11
Amber Murphy (10)	12
Max Wiltshire	13
Sophia Parton (10)	14
Molly Hitchin (9)	15
Archie Carmichael-Johns (10)	16

Castleford Park Junior Academy, Castleford

Poppy Johnson (8)	17
Oliver Peters (8)	18
Lexie Martin-Smith (7)	20
Ethan McLoughlin (9)	21
A Dean (9)	22
Alex Catch (8)	23
Hettie Hobman (8)	24
Sophie Macdonald (7)	25
Esmae Barker (7)	26

Copthorne CE Junior School, Copthorne

Frank Still (7)	27
Louie Melton-Ball (8)	28
Declan Sylva	30
Ava James (7)	31
Esmé Hulme	32
Emelia Holman (9)	33
Lara Mitchell	34
Harry Whittaker (9)	35
Zachary McDonald (8)	36
Amelia Jimpson (7)	37
Jake Cooke (9)	38
Jessica Searle (10)	39
Lola Hulme	40
Louis Whyman	41
Aiden Njenga (10)	42

Hewens Primary School, Hayes

Aaron Rao (7)	43
Phoebie-Mai Hammett (8)	44
Nancy Ordia (9)	46
Rui Degun (7)	47
Natalia Dolecka (8)	48
Mani Sagoo (8)	49
Harady Yonis (7)	50
Laurentiu Perju (9)	51
Mahi Dhillon (8)	52
Mira Dhillon (8)	53
Zarni Aye (8)	54
Isaiah Kyagaba (7)	55
Denisha Duggal (8)	56
Syriah Green (8)	57
Aaliya Hassan	58

Osheli Wickramasinghe (8)	59
Scarlett Ruff (8)	60
Sienna Takhar (8)	61
Isabella Vrakettas (7)	62
Merenna Semuthu Jayaratne (8)	63
Devan Bhalsod (7)	64
Ailey Shannon Wijesinghe (7)	65
Toby Luff (8)	66
Rajpaul Sagoo (9)	67
Rashmi Pakeerathan (8)	68
Thlil Chowdhury (7)	69
Gurshan Dhaliwal (8)	70
Daniel East (8)	71
Angad Singh (7)	72
Laraya Watson (7)	73
Sahar Jaseem (7)	74

Joydens Wood Junior School, Wilmington

Olivia Bevan-Brown (8)	75
Alana Bharucha (11)	76
Eli Tobias (10)	78
Stephanie Hillier (8)	79
Yoanna Nikolova (10)	80
Babafunto Adeyinka-Ojo (8)	81
Riley Dannatt (9)	82
Orla Porter (9)	83
Maci Jones (7)	84
Liam Dimitriadis (8)	85
Ava Brooks (9)	86
Sienna Askew	87
Alice Jarrett (8)	88
Henry Chapman (7)	89
Michael Nikulin (8)	90
Heashika Sivakumar (7)	91
Harshika Sivakumar (10)	92
Rio Merja (8)	93

Oasis Academy Watermead, Sheffield

Prince Gachogu (10)	94
Billie Machin (11)	95

Yara Tahir (11)	96
David Moraru (10)	97
Mohammed Tarram (11)	98
Shannelle Kelly (10)	99

Peel Park Primary School, Accrington

Evie-Grace Bailey (7)	100
Charli Molloy (7)	102
Paige Carlton (8)	103
Amir Mufleh (7)	104
Melissa Courtney (7)	105
Ruby Pilkington (8)	106
Danny Walker (7)	107
Jordan McCormack (8)	108
Mia Johnstone (7)	109
Summer Crabtree (7)	110
Shanum Zaheer (7)	111
Erin Daniels (7)	112
Tyler Gibson (7)	113
Ramzaan Ali (7)	114
Sophia Hosker (7)	115

Singlewell Primary School, Gravesend

Ryan Moore (10)	116
Anya Ceka (8)	118
Yannis Kamdem (9)	119
Henry Shanley (7)	120
Anayah Chakravorty (8)	121
Emily Bishop (6)	122
Naveah Henry (10)	123
Judah Mangundu (6)	124
Albie Turner (7)	125
Joseph Brussee (8)	126
Hollie Smith (6)	127
Sienna Roberts (7)	128
Joel Gyateng (9)	129
Ashley Payne (7)	130
Olive Owen-Harvey (9)	131
Rhys Hutchinson (7)	132
Aston Moody-Gbasai (6)	133

Cameron Bennett (9)	134
Ella Parkinson (9)	135
Alba Young (4)	136
Elsie Olatoye (5)	137
Max Cavey (4)	138
Finley Mepstead (4)	139
Cerys Jarvis (5)	140
Milana Bomiriyage (5)	141

Southbank International School Kensington, Notting Hill

Daksha Mishra (9)	142
Frida Gauder (9)	145
Mason Sheckman (10)	146
Luisa Nutz Wloch (9)	148
Sadie Tomlin (10)	150
Ella Piro (10)	152
Chance Coughlin	154

St Anne's CE Primary School, Oldland Common

Imogen King (10)	156
Amelia Woodland (10)	157
Alex Wood (10)	158
James Rigby (10)	160
Brayden Hembrough (10)	161
Colby Walker (11)	162
Poppy Forbes (10)	163
Danilo Amato (10)	164
Mollie Bateman (11)	165
Katie Phillips (10)	166
Temini Ezobi (11)	167
Andrew Tresise (11)	168
Lily-Mai Williams (11)	169
Summer Currey (10)	170
Tom Gregory Fear (10)	171
Amela Levett (10)	172
Myla Bliss (10)	173
Lotti Butler (10)	174
Alana Spiller (10)	175
Ava Humphries (11)	176
Lauren Smith (10)	177

Noah S (10)	178
Maisie Townsend (10)	179
Oliver Savage (10)	180
Brooke Lamb-Collins (10)	181
Ben Kuciak (11)	182
Priya Ludwell (10)	183
Elise Bishop (10)	184
Amelia Stokes (10)	185
Daniel Darby (10)	186
Ruby Bristow (11)	187
Abi Lowman (10)	188
Harvey Drew (10)	189
Freya Kelly (10)	190
George Hillier (10)	191

St Anthony's Catholic Primary School, Kingshurst

Darci Yates-Henry (10)	192
Ana Sandhu (8)	194
Lois Wilson (7)	195
Rosie Brannigan (7)	196
Bobbie O'Mara (8)	197
Julia Urbanska (8)	198

St Edward's Royal Free Ecumenical Middle School, Windsor

Elliott Marsden (9)	199
Elena Littlewood (11)	200
Liliana Baxendale (10)	203
Ayinoor Murray (9)	204
Rose Jackson (10)	206
Averil Newton (11)	207
Charlotte Kieren (11)	208
Willow Banasko-Lawson (10)	209
Chloe Balla (11)	210
Millie Mander (9)	211
Maya Trevisan (9)	212

Thames Primary Academy, Blackpool

Minahil Waqas	213
Thomas Hill (10)	214
Florence Brown	215
Najwa Raisa	216
Lexi Glover (9)	217
Hallie Taylor	218
Gabriel Bennett (9)	219

THE POEMS

Penguin Persona

My mind is like a lightbulb
But my memory is like a never-ending hole
I can't remember what I had for my last meal
But in maths, I'm as slick as a seal
I love to grow things like peas
But I never really did like cheese
I have the same diet as my favourite animal
But to fish, I'm a straight-up cannibal

I've always wanted to have a penguin as a pet
But I've never really wanted to clean up their mess
I'm not really a sporty bloke
But I have a killer breaststroke
To sum me up in one little thing
I really am just a clever penguin!

Felix Cole (10)
Aldbury CE Primary & Nursery School, Aldbury

This Is Me!

I think cricket
Is as easy as dunking a biscuit
Football, you ask?
Not actually a hard task

I have a family of three and six
Something I cannot fix
I have a brother who is super annoying
Personally, I think he is really intimidating

I have a fast and quick mind
But I am always very kind
Maths is my biggest power in life
But personally, no subject is a strife

I'm not too bad at tennis
But I am quite a menace*
I always hit the ball miles
Bet anyone wouldn't take me for trials

On a good day, I'll lead your way
On a bad one, I am a sunken bay

English is a very lovely thing to do
Science is cool too
RE is of religions and their gods
But I don't believe in the odds

Can swim back, front and breast
I think I am the best
Although I am not
I can always plot**

So this is me after all that
I am really not that flat
I can be sweet, I can be sour
Really depending on the hour
But at the very end
I will always have the best friends!

* with the ball
** on how to get better

Eric Niblock (11)
Aldbury CE Primary & Nursery School, Aldbury

This Is Me

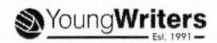

A creature of only land, not sea
It can swim but cannot breathe

Her name is a type of flower
Thinking of heights makes her cower

She loves stand up surfing in the ocean
She always puts in a lot of devotion

She has quite a good passion
It's a nice stylist fashion

She is sweet, she is sour
Always depending on the hour

She has a nice trait of making you smile
But not always, don't worry, it's done after a while

And yes, likes to swim in the sea
But hey, I guess that's just me!

Rose Jenkins
Aldbury CE Primary & Nursery School, Aldbury

This Is Me!

Having fun
Having a run
I'm sweet, I'm sour
It really depends on the hour
I'll tower above people
I'll cower below
I'll leap around
When City bag yet one more
Will we get another?

Sport is me
But relaxing I like to do
Football I do
I pick up lots of clues
A mathematician
Not an electrician.

Ben Woodhams
Aldbury CE Primary & Nursery School, Aldbury

This Is Me

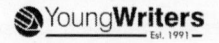

What has two legs
And can slide across the dance floors?
Write along silk pages
Burst her heart out with kindness and laughter
Snuggle through cold winters
Go absolutely crazy when it's her birthday
Cry when another cries
Protest for a change
And fight dragons in her sleep
Amber Verinder
That is me!

Amber Verinder (10)
Aldbury CE Primary & Nursery School, Aldbury

This Is Me

Respectful, kind
A super-fast person
PE is my superpower
But art makes me cower

Sometimes I'm in a bad mood
But my friends cheer me up
I turn my frown upside down

I am honest and always
A happy person normally
My chaotic friends cheer me up

This is me!

Mitchell Phillips (10)
Aldbury CE Primary & Nursery School, Aldbury

I Am A...

Sports player
Courageous cricketer
Food lover
I don't know where my memory goes
The cricket square is where I like most
I'm an online player
I have an interest in the medical fight
My pets are part of my life
My friends and family are what I love most
This is me.

Maxwell MacGregor (9)
Aldbury CE Primary & Nursery School, Aldbury

Me

Mind of a fox
As strong as an ox
Leap of a lemur
Swim of a swan
I am a good grower
But not a thrower
Acting, practising, timing
Climbing, flying (in planes)
I am sweet, I am sour
Depending on the hour
Maths is my power
But sometimes makes me cower.

Leon Niblock (9)
Aldbury CE Primary & Nursery School, Aldbury

This Is Me

I am afraid of the dark
I like a good lark
I play in the park

I like singing
Like a dolphin at swimming
I am ace at swinging

I like a good race
Have a funny face
Live in a place
Where I tie my lace

That's who I am.

Henrietta French (9)
Aldbury CE Primary & Nursery School, Aldbury

Oliver

O nline gamer
L aughs and make jokes to my buddies
I love football, tennis and rounders, it's so fun
V ery kind to my best friends and family
E nergetic and enthusiastic
R especting others and treating people fairly.

Oliver Speck
Aldbury CE Primary & Nursery School, Aldbury

This Is Me

T he best sleeper
H appy gamer
I ntelligent as a monkey
S uper as school

I maginative as a grandma
S easide is my favourite place

M aker of fun
E xcellent at caring for all.

Amber Murphy (10)
Aldbury CE Primary & Nursery School, Aldbury

This Is Me

Football is great, I love to score
Although my friends call me a wild boar
I may be crazy but I'm definitely not lazy
I'm always running, even though life has
Its ups and downs
I also like art and that's not hard to like.

Max Wiltshire
Aldbury CE Primary & Nursery School, Aldbury

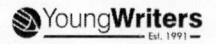

I Am A...

T ennis player
H alloween lover
I ce skater
S wimming star

I ncredibly early riser
S uper gymnast

M aths hero
E nthusiastic person.

Sophia Parton (10)
Aldbury CE Primary & Nursery School, Aldbury

This Is Me

Smiley
Untidy
Brilliant striker
Extraordinary hiker
Dog's mother
Sloth lover
Idea maker
Cake baker
Likes Hawaiian pizza
I'm sure you'd
Like to meet her.

Molly Hitchin (9)
Aldbury CE Primary & Nursery School, Aldbury

I Am

An athletic runner
Funny, kind
Chocolate lover
Crisp lover
Game player
Heavy sleeper
Super swimmer
This is who I am
This is me.

Archie Carmichael-Johns (10)
Aldbury CE Primary & Nursery School, Aldbury

Princess Poppy

I like to dance and sometimes sing
Dancing is my favourite thing
Jump up high, bob down low
These are my favourite moves, you know
I have super long princess hair
I like to share and always care
When I'm sad, I like to colour
It makes everything not as duller
My dream is to become a dance teacher
I know it will because I'm a believer
I'm Princess Poppy
Dance is my hobby
Turquoise is a super colour
But I also like multicolour
Come one everybody, let's have a dance
It's always good to take a chance.

Poppy Johnson (8)
Castleford Park Junior Academy, Castleford

This Is Me

Eat your breakfast
Get dressed
Make your bed

Have you brushed your teeth?

Reading
TTRS
Spellings, we need ten

Put your shoes on
Oliver! No!

Good job
Well done
Yes, you can

Did you have a good day?

Okay
Maybe
Not now

Oliver... Eat your tea!

Hug time
Tickle time
Me time

Get changed

It's a long day being me!

Oliver Peters (8)
Castleford Park Junior Academy, Castleford

All About Me

Hands to help with eyes to see
I'm very happy with all of me
Ears to hear with feet so free
I'm very happy with all of me
Nose to smell with legs to climb a tree
I'm very happy with all of me
I am growing as big as can be
I'm very happy with all of me
Brown is my hair, blue is my eyes
I'm seven years old and just the right size
My name is Lexie and as you can see
I'm very happy to be me!

Lexie Martin-Smith (7)
Castleford Park Junior Academy, Castleford

Bob

When I was born, I had no name
So, Bob, it was until I became
The boy that stands before you now
The boy who hugs and laugh out loud
My favourite things are maths and science
I also have a karate licence
Sweets and cakes and PJ days
To ride a bike and play my games
In the future, I might be a super swimmer
Or referee.

Ethan McLoughlin (9)
Castleford Park Junior Academy, Castleford

Adoption

A forever family, loving and giving
D evoted to me, unconditionally
O nward together on life's exciting journey
P ositivity in abundance
T rying my best in all I do
I love my life, it makes me smile
O pen and honest and how proud I feel
N aturally resilient and strong.

A Dean (9)
Castleford Park Junior Academy, Castleford

My World

Playing Pokémon
And Super Slimetastic
Glorious games
Using ideas, inventing
And marvelling at maths
Caring for creatures
And noticing nature
All around me
Family fun
And dazzling days out.

Alex Catch (8)
Castleford Park Junior Academy, Castleford

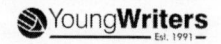

Me
A kennings poem

Daydreams
Ice creams
Loves swimming
Christmas trimming
Family forever
Fall out never
Brownies meeting
Trick or treating
Roblox player
Caravan stayer
Adores spaghetti
I am Hettie.

Hettie Hobman (8)
Castleford Park Junior Academy, Castleford

I Love Bugs

I love the outdoors
And things that have paws
I love bugs and slugs
Give me a bunch of hugs
See them crawl on the wall
I am so tall
Bugs make me smile
Like a sweet child.

Sophie Macdonald (7)
Castleford Park Junior Academy, Castleford

About Esmae

E xcellent
S assy
M ature
A mazing
E nergetic.

Esmae Barker (7)
Castleford Park Junior Academy, Castleford

How To Make The Perfect Me

I will put into my heart...
A sprinkle of happiness mixed with some hugs

I will put into my mind...
To be a famous footballer who uses his voice to make everyone kind to each other

I will put into my actions...
To share food with those who are poor and can't afford food for themselves

I will put into my world...
Kindness, theme parks and people who don't litter

My life will be built upon...
A family who care about me

I want to be remembered for...
Helping keep children who don't have food healthy.

Frank Still (7)
Copthorne CE Junior School, Copthorne

How To Make The Perfect Me

I will put into my heart...
To make everyone happy and smiling
Kindness for everyone in the world
Love my family and pizza!

I will put into my mind...
Never-ending football training for two hours
Happiness to learn maths and writing
To never give up

I will put into my actions...
I will keep practising to get better and better
I will care for friends and family

I will put into my world...
I will have ice cream and pizza every Friday
Kindness for everyone

My life will be built upon...
My caring family and friends who are always there for me

I want to be remembered for...
Being an amazing footballer and incredible friend to everyone

Louie Melton-Ball (8)
Copthorne CE Junior School, Copthorne

Fortnite, Eat, Sleep, Game

Fortnite, eat, sleep, game
I might be tall, but I excel in school
My favourite sport is football, how about yours?
I moonwalk my way to victory
Science is not my thing but times tables is where
I should be
I want to go to Jupiter, but I might get smarter
I'm crazy because that's my personality
I came 50th in a solo cash-cup
I'm a boss at Fortnite, so what's up?
I can be troublesome, but when I focus
I can do anything.

Declan Sylva
Copthorne CE Junior School, Copthorne

How To Make Love In This Beautiful World

I will put into my heart, love and kindness everywhere around the world
I will put into my mind, all the things that I've seen that are beautiful
I will put into my attitude, good words and behaviour
I will put into my world, more flowers, happiness, my whole family and the sun
My world will be built upon love, animals, teachers and family
I want to be remembered for helping people and doing good for my school.

Ava James (7)
Copthorne CE Junior School, Copthorne

This Is Me!

I'm arty, I am kind and a little bit shy
Even though I don't know why
I have brown hair and blue eyes
Brighter than the seven skies
When I was one, I had no hair
When I was two, I did not share
When I was three, I got stung by a bee
When I was four, I lived in a tree
When I was five, I played the drums
When I was six, I ate some plums
When I was seven, I had a cat
When I was eight, the cat got fat!

Esmé Hulme
Copthorne CE Junior School, Copthorne

This Is Me!

I'm kind, I'm caring
I'm very good at sharing
I have blue eyes, brown hair
I play the game very fair
My favourite colour is blue, just like the sea
I love little tiny bumblebees
I have two younger siblings, I'm the oldest child
I'm not going to lie they go a bit wild!
I'm sometimes happy, I'm sometimes sad
But my sisters make me go mad!
Anyway, this is me!

Emelia Holman (9)
Copthorne CE Junior School, Copthorne

This Is Me!

When I was one, I loved my bum
When I was two, I learnt to poo
When I was three, I did a pee
When I was four, I broke the law
When I was five, I learnt to drive
When I was six, I met Little Mix
When I was seven, I went to heaven
When I was eight, I learnt to skate
When I was nine, I did a crime
When I was ten, I wouldn't do that again.

Lara Mitchell
Copthorne CE Junior School, Copthorne

This Is Me!

A kennings poem

I am a...
Football player
Nugget lover
Friendly face
Funny mate
Tree-planter
Planet restorer
Sports player
Pizza maker
But football is my jam
Guitar guru
Joke shouter
Family lover
Annoying brother
Early riser
Nintendo player
Dog trainer
Loyal friend
And that is who I am.

Harry Whittaker (9)
Copthorne CE Junior School, Copthorne

This Is Me

This is me, kind, helpful, fun in the sun
Helpful when the moon falls
If you're sad, I will make you shine bright
like the sun
Sizzling sun as I have fun
In the dark, I will play football in the stars
Sporty, running, cycling and football. This is me!
Mum running with me. This is me!
Every day playing football. This is me!

Zachary McDonald (8)
Copthorne CE Junior School, Copthorne

How To Make The Perfect Me

I will put into my heart, love and my family
I will put into my mind, my brother and sister
I will put into my attitude, kindness and helpfulness
I will put into my world, kindness for my family and pets
My world will be built upon friendship, friends and family
And I want to be remembered for helping people around me.

Amelia Jimpson (7)
Copthorne CE Junior School, Copthorne

Be Free Like Me!

I have brown whipped coffee eyes like the autumn leaves
I feel free when I'm with the beautiful streams
I don't know what I would do without the trees
My beat goes hard with the waves in the sea
I feel alive when the wild calls me
Take a look at the trees, maybe you'll see me.

Jake Cooke (9)
Copthorne CE Junior School, Copthorne

Magnificent Me
A kennings poem

Cake scorcher,
Cookie lover,
Chip chomper,
Milkshake chugger,
Sofa sleeper,
Armchair napper,
Teddy cuddler,
Pool bomber,
Pencil hogger,
Story writer,
Book devourer,
Dog patter,

Overall sincere soul sister!

Jessica Searle (10)
Copthorne CE Junior School, Copthorne

Magic Me
A kennings poem

Family lover
Family hugger
Kitchen cooker
Water guzzler
Pool splasher
All-day snacker
Playground player
Road jogger
Butterfly painter
All-day dozer
All-round great sister.

Lola Hulme
Copthorne CE Junior School, Copthorne

Louis' Life

A kennings poem

Cricket player
Football kicker
Liverpool lover
Bike rider
Race runner
Food devourer
Duck carer
Chicken feeder
Fun producer
School attender
Problem solver
Book reader.

Louis Whyman
Copthorne CE Junior School, Copthorne

Marvellous Me

A kennings poem

Chocolate muncher
Food gobbler
Bed snoozer
Couch hugger
Leave my stuff alone
PS5 gamer
Ace shooter
Gaming lover
Goal smasher
Horrible smiler
All-round great brother.

Aiden Njenga (10)
Copthorne CE Junior School, Copthorne

My School Routine

I wake up in the morning, do my brush,
Eat my breakfast and then rush.

I reach my school a little late,
But thank goodness, I find an open gate.

When I enter the class, see all the happy faces,
I then realise, learning here is never an impasses.

At break time, we play lots of games,
Outdoor in summer and indoor in rain.

Then we troop back to the class,
To do more interesting tasks.

Finally, the most awaited time comes,
When we pack our bags and head for home.

Aaron Rao (7)
Hewens Primary School, Hayes

Phoebie's Autism Days

I am Phoebie-Mai
And here is my day to day
I struggle to read and write
But I do love to play
I have two special friends
Scarlett and Kai
I love them more than cherry pie
I struggle going in every day
Then I see Miss Johnson
Which brightens my day
I am not as clever as many, I know
But I have perfect ideas, so there you go
I love to play Roblox and YouTube too
I love a good sing-a-long and music too
I do like routine and time out too
I know sometimes you think I don't listen
But Miss Johnson, I really do!
I am eight and in my own world
But Mummy says I can be whatever I want to be
Sometimes I'm sad and sometimes I cry
But I don't like it either way

It's not my fault, it's who I am
I'm just learning maths, it can be fun
Thanks, Miss Johnson, for making it awesome
Mummy and Daddy love me for who I am
I am Phoebie-Mai and it's who I am
I rock special needs
So I guess that's me!

Phoebie-Mai Hammett (8)
Hewens Primary School, Hayes

Nice And Fabulous Me!

N ice, fabulous, gorgeous and pretty, that's me
I n sad times, I may cry but that doesn't ruin my face
C an I be ugly? Never, because I'm pretty, that's me
E ver pretty and gorgeous

A s an angel
N icely formed and created, one to eight, coming up to nine
D ivine and gorgeous all over, that's me

F abulous day and night
A s beautiful as a rose
B etter than the best
U nassuming
L oving
O n the front cover of a magazine
U nstoppable
S assy

M arvellous
E ver fabulous, that's me!

Nancy Ordia (9)
Hewens Primary School, Hayes

The Things That Make Me Me!

Here's a quick recipe
If you'd like to try
To make a cute little girl
Who's really not that shy

Add some sugar and some sparkle, some glitter and some honey
All the wonderful things to make her yummy
Add some kindness and some strength, some courage and hope
I promise you, this is not a joke
The last step is easy, it doesn't take that long
One ingredient left to add, you really can't go wrong
The key to making me is adding lots of love
Once it's all been added and looks a little gooey
You've made the perfect recipe to have your own Rui!

Rui Degun (7)
Hewens Primary School, Hayes

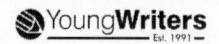

Me Being Active

My name is Natalia and I am an active girl
I never stop moving because I always run around
I play football every day
I want to be a football trainer because... why not?
I am as quick as a flash
My dream is to be an amazing athlete
And win medals at the Olympics
I go swimming every Tuesday
I enjoy some fun swimming
Sometimes, I go with my grandad
For a peaceful swim in the week
I have learnt and am still learning
A lot of ways to swim
So you see, I never stop moving
On land or in water, I never stop
So... this is me!

Natalia Dolecka (8)
Hewens Primary School, Hayes

I Am Mani

My name is Mani,
I enjoy the taste of honey.
My talent is to talk,
And I love to run and walk.

I do a martial art called karate,
I also love to help everybody.
I absorb everything like a sponge constantly,
Mighty, majestic me!

I have an awesome dream career,
As I want to be an electrical engineer.
I am as wild as a cheetah,
And as smart as an encyclopedia.

I am a falcon flying through the air,
So very extraordinare!
My favourite colour is red,
Follow me and you won't be misled.

Mani Sagoo (8)
Hewens Primary School, Hayes

This Is Me

My name is Harady
And I like to play football with my friend
My favourite food is pears, apples, oranges and green apples
And I like to help people who need my help
And if you need help I will be there to help in a flash
And if you need help in the night I will be there
Do you know what is my favourite?
My favourite thing is sweets
I like to eat sweets
Some sweets are healthy
And my dream is to become a doctor
When I'm feeling better and if I am feeling sad and angry
I like to help.

Harady Yonis (7)
Hewens Primary School, Hayes

My Feelings

These make me cheerful:
Sunshine on the sea,
Birthday parties,
Presents
And my favourite food for tea.

These things make me sad:
A grey and gloomy day,
Unkind words and unkind looks,
When friends just walk away.

These things make me frightened:
Thunderstorms that go *boom!*
Crawly bugs and creepy dreams
And shadows around my room.

These things make me calm:
A smile from a friend,
Sleepy bedtime stories
With a very happy end.

Laurentiu Perju (9)
Hewens Primary School, Hayes

Mahi Dhillon

M y favourite food is pepperoni pizza
A lligators are my least favourite animal
H ello Neighbour is my favourite game
I am a courageous girl

D olphins are my favourite animal
H ill parks are my favourite places
I am an intelligent child
L earning mathematics is my favourite hobby
L ife is important to me
O n the way to different places, I like to dance
N uggets and French fries are the best!

Mahi Dhillon (8)
Hewens Primary School, Hayes

Mira Dhillon

M y favourite hobby is playing with my school friends
I am a courageous girl
R aya is my favourite movie
A iley is my best friend

D ogs are my favourite animals when they're calm
H alloween is one of the best festivals
I love vanilla ice cream
L earning maths is the best
L ife skills are important to save lives
O n long drives, I like to sleep
N uggets and potato chips are delicious.

Mira Dhillon (8)
Hewens Primary School, Hayes

All About Me!

My name is Zarni and I like to play
A game called FNF every single day

I'm a September baby, yeah that's true
I go on my bodyboard, that's what I do

Now, let's talk about my family
My sister is eleven
My parents were born around 1987

When I grow up, I want to be an awesome astronaut
Training under the sea

My name is Zarni and you'll never forget
I need to eat my chicken nuggets!

Zarni Aye (8)
Hewens Primary School, Hayes

All About Me!

Do you know a seven-year-old tall superhero
Who likes shepherd's pie
And maple syrup on his pancakes?
A great football fun

Who wants to be Prime Minister
When he grows up

He feels better when he
Reads a Marvel or Transformer book

Who is a happy person
And has a good sense of humour

He admires his dad
Because he takes him to school
And he's very helpful
That's Isaiah.

Isaiah Kyagaba (7)
Hewens Primary School, Hayes

This Is Me

Roses are red
Violets are blue
I am going to tell all about me to you
I love to read
I believe in doing good deeds
My earrings are gold
I am eight years old
My eyes are the colour of hazel
And in the sun they dazzle
My mum says I am a sweetheart
Full of kindness in my heart
I love to study in school
And swim in the pool
My favourite is maths
And I love to take hot baths
This is me.

Denisha Duggal (8)
Hewens Primary School, Hayes

Out By The Light Of The Moon

To be out by the light of the moon
It has to be afternoon
When the lights are out
I wander and wander about
The thieves on streets
Tickle my feet
While creeping around
Not making a sound
I hide behind a tree
Letting the foxes be
The squeaking mice at night
The spiky hedgehogs who love the night sky
The warm wolves that love the berries
That grow only in the moonlight
All love to be out.

Syriah Green (8)
Hewens Primary School, Hayes

The Heart-Touching Poem

It was that one moment
So I ask you to let me go with you
Into those hidden parts of you
And we will discover who you are
If you always try your best
Then you'll never have to wonder
About when you could have done
If you have all your powers and if your best
Was not as good as you hoped it would be
You still could say I gave today all that I had in me
You are the best person in your life.

Aaliya Hassan
Hewens Primary School, Hayes

The Things That Osheli Makes Better

I am counting down till Saturday
Because that's my fun day
I do gymnastics on this day
Because it makes me happy

I like riding the bike to the park
But I forgot to wear my mask
I heard a dog bark
Then we came back before it got dark

I like playing football with my brother
He is slow and I am faster
My mum saw it and makes me happier
And that makes me feel better.

Osheli Wickramasinghe (8)
Hewens Primary School, Hayes

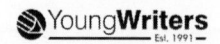

I Am Me!

My name is Scarlett, it means the colour red
I love reading to go on adventures before I go to bed
I have lots of lovely, funny, kind friends that mean a lot to me
I am as kind and sharing as can be
I love my mummy, daddy and my brothers
I love chocolate, cats, gaming and lots of others
I love the colour purple and wish I was a unicorn so free
This is my poem all about me.

Scarlett Ruff (8)
Hewens Primary School, Hayes

It's All About Me

I'm happy, I'm funny, I'm loving and I'm sassy
I like blue, I like pink, I like purple because I'm classy

I'm prettier than the sun when that day has just begun
I don't mind jogging, I just don't like to run

I give great hugs, I'm smart, I like watermelon in my tummy
It's super-duper yummy and I really love my mummy!

Sienna Takhar (8)
Hewens Primary School, Hayes

My Dog And The Lark

My dog sat on a log
In the middle of the park
A bird flew down beside him
It was a little lark
They went on a swing
nd the lark started to sing
Then my dog started to bark
They had so much fun
My dog found a bun
And shared it with the lark
They both licked their lips
And water they sipped
Friends forever they stayed.

Isabella Vrakettas (7)
Hewens Primary School, Hayes

All About Myself

Being myself is great, I get to do everything
I get to play, I get to work throughout the joyful day

I like days, rainy and sunny, I don't care
I just love the days that pass by

I'm great and proud for who I am
My name just says it all
Every blink, every smile makes me happy
I'm happy for who I am right now.

Merenna Semuthu Jayaratne (8)
Hewens Primary School, Hayes

Football Is My Favourite Game!

Football is my favourite game
I run like the wind as my team win
I love to play football in a team
And to play for Manchester United is my dream
I love it when people shout my name
As I continue to play this beautiful game
The best thing about football
Is when the fans roar
Every time I score
Football is my favourite game.

Devan Bhalsod (7)
Hewens Primary School, Hayes

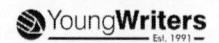

My Inside Self

You might think I'm just a person
Well, I'm a lot of things
I can change the world
From sobbing to happiness
From happiness to loving
I'll make everyone have a great mindset
I'll never let anyone down
Even my friends
As well as my name
I am the light to this life.

Ailey Shannon Wijesinghe (7)
Hewens Primary School, Hayes

I'm Toby

T otally athletic
O bviously energetic
B est of all, friendly
Y oshi is the best

L ots of love to give
U nderstanding always
F unny nature
F antastic personality

And most all, I'm me!

Toby Luff (8)
Hewens Primary School, Hayes

I Am Rajpaul!

R espectful to my elders,
A ctive while practising karate,
J olly with a smile on my face,
P atient while waiting for my brother,
A rtistic because I like drawing,
U ltimate like a superhero,
L ively as a grasshopper!

Rajpaul Sagoo (9)
Hewens Primary School, Hayes

Guess Who?

She's a girl
She loves burgers
Her name starts with 'R'
And ends with 'E'
It's like Michelle but I bet you'll never see
She's my best friend
And she's amazing as can be
Who is she?

Rashmi Pakeerathan (8)
Hewens Primary School, Hayes

Tricky Riddles

If you drop me off a cliff
I seem to be fine
But if you drop me in water, I die
What am I?

I am a paper.

If you drop me, I break
But if you smile, I smile back
What am I?

I am a mirror.

Thlil Chowdhury (7)
Hewens Primary School, Hayes

Football Champ

I am a football champ
I went to football camp
I love to play football
I can play days all
I go to the playground
Where my friends can be found
Football is my favourite game
Football can give me fame.

Gurshan Dhaliwal (8)
Hewens Primary School, Hayes

Daniel

D aily drinking my diet coke
A n awesome life I live
N othing beats taekwondo
I love it more than anything
E verything is golden
L ife is going to take me far.

Daniel East (8)
Hewens Primary School, Hayes

Football

F un and competitive
O utstanding
O ptimistic
T hrilling
B est sport ever
A merica's game
L eadership
L oyalty.

Angad Singh (7)
Hewens Primary School, Hayes

Affirmation Of Laraya

I am **L** ovely
I am **A** mazing
I am **R** espectful
I am **A** thletic, I love sport
I am **Y** oung, I love to have fun
I am **A** lways grateful.

Laraya Watson (7)
Hewens Primary School, Hayes

This Is Me

I am as colourful as a rainbow
I am as cute as liquorice
I am as fast as a cheetah
I am totally cool and amazing
I am as tall as a tree.

Sahar Jaseem (7)
Hewens Primary School, Hayes

This Is Me

O scar is my lovely, helpful brother, He is as crazy as a superhero
L iving in Joydens Wood, we soon will be
I love eating big, crunchy, juicy chocolate strawberries
V ery happy I am when I do my tap dancing a lot
I sle of Wight is where we go on holiday to see our family
A black Labrador who is really soft called Tilly, is our dog. She is as cute as a button

G ood at running and throwing, I am
R iding my fast, pink bike is lots of fun. I am as speedy as a cheetah
A nimals are my favourite things
C arrots are a nice healthy snack in the middle of the afternoon for me
E lephants are one of my favourite animals. They are as tall as a tree.

Olivia Bevan-Brown (8)
Joydens Wood Junior School, Wilmington

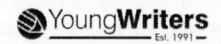

Alana

The dictionary describes me as...
Loving
Amazingly beautiful
Sweetly sarcastic
Sassy yet fearless
Independent and smart
Successful young woman

Other cultures describe me as...
Awakening
Fair
Beautiful
Childlike
Summarising this all up
I am a playful childish character

My friends and family describe me as...
Smart
Independent
A leader
Pretty
Mature

Cheeky
Thoughtful
And fortunate to know

I describe myself as...
- **A** smart, sensible girl
- **L** oving to those I care about
- **A** wesome at understanding others
- **N** ew challenges help me succeed
- **A** friendly, social person

This is me!

Alana Bharucha (11)
Joydens Wood Junior School, Wilmington

My Pencil And Me!

The flow of my pencil is like a fish swimming
in the ocean
As the pencil stroke in a synchronised motion
The paper touches my pencil with elegance
and pride
As the lead of my pencil strokes the paper
as it glides
Whether thick or as thin as a twig
My pencil flows whether small lines or big
Like a dog free from its lead or a happy old pig
with no help in need
My anger shows in the pencil's flow and my joy
scribbles in the need to go
Drawing with a pencil is all I love
Even when times are hard and tough...

Eli Tobias (10)
Joydens Wood Junior School, Wilmington

This Is Me, Stephanie!

I am clumsy and fall over
Whilst I'm looking for a four-leaf clover
I am eager and tiny too
I am friendly and will play with you
I play the piano, the music is fun
Then I play outside in the sun
I am caring, kind and warm
When I'm with my friends I like to perform
I am scary on Halloween saying, "Trick or treatie?"
When I get home I'll share my sweetie
I am sporty and love swimming
I enjoy it because I am winning
I am smart, funny and kind
I will not be redefined.

Stephanie Hillier (8)
Joydens Wood Junior School, Wilmington

This Is Me!

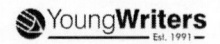

I am blue
I dance with the ocean
I sing with the bluebirds
Eating blueberries
Makes me have a summer emotion!
I am green
I hide in the trees
I observe nature grow
I love to be me!
I am red
Like flames, I am angry when I am unheard
I skip through a meadow of roses
My best friend is a pretty ladybird.
I am yellow
As yellow as a busy bumblebee
You can see my silhouette in the sun
I'm running through a sunflower field
You can't catch me!

Yoanna Nikolova (10)
Joydens Wood Junior School, Wilmington

This Is Who I Am

T his is who I am
H opeful, faithful
I mpressive enough to catch your attention
S oft-hearted and emotional

I am an intellectual
S o don't mess with me

W hen I am in school, I am in a happy mood
H ealthy and ready to play
O rganised every time

I am tall

A lmost a giant
M y best friend is nice.

Babafunto Adeyinka-Ojo (8)
Joydens Wood Junior School, Wilmington

This Is Me

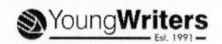

This is me
I don't like getting up early
Except on weekends
I love my technology
I'm always happy
Hanging around with Hammy
Hammy is my hamster
He's always on the run
Scoffing down all his treats
He's always such fun
I love playing football
Rinning down the wing
Sometimes when we win
We do a little sing
This is me
And my name is Riley.

Riley Dannatt (9)
Joydens Wood Junior School, Wilmington

This Is Life

T iny fennec foxes are my favourite animal
H ugging my family is the best
I love my friends and family
S easide is my happy place

I love school and my teacher is the best. She is so kind
S piders are my worst fear

M e and my family always play games
E rin is my sister, she is the best.

Orla Porter (9)
Joydens Wood Junior School, Wilmington

This Is All About Me...

My name is Maci Jones
What I love best in the whole world
Is my dog, Billie
She is a puppy and very, very silly
I like to help my mum to bake
My favourite is chocolate cake
We love to go camping at the seaside
I play on the seafront rides
I miss my brother, Ollie
He's at uni but that's okay
I have stolen his bedroom.

Maci Jones (7)
Joydens Wood Junior School, Wilmington

My Name Is Liam, Yes It Is...

My name is Liam, yes it is...
In Minecraft, I'm a whizz
I was a noob, pro then hacker
Which also rhymes with cracker
One day, I'll be a Minecraft god

My name is Liam, yes it is...
And when it comes to niceness, I fizz
I also enjoy reading books
With plenty of hooks
One day I'll even write my own book!

Liam Dimitriadis (8)
Joydens Wood Junior School, Wilmington

Football

F avourite team about to play
O ver excited, I'm a little nervous
O n the pitch, waiting for the whistle
T he match has started
B all flying down the pitch
A quick kick towards the goal
L eft-hand corner and it's in the net
L oads of cheers from our fans and family.

Ava Brooks (9)
Joydens Wood Junior School, Wilmington

This Is Me

My name is Sienna and I'm a girl
I like to dance, I like to twirl
I love my dog, he is the best
He makes me smile more than the rest
My eyes are brown, my hair is long
And I like to sing along
I like the beach and days in the sun
I like to smile and always have fun.

Sienna Askew
Joydens Wood Junior School, Wilmington

This Is Me

I am a...
Art lover
Book reader
Cuddle monster
Great friend
Pizza eater
Perfect painter
Messy daughter
Book writer

In love with unicorns
Love everything with a shine
Great sister, I hope that's true
And most of all, I am...
Me!

Alice Jarrett (8)
Joydens Wood Junior School, Wilmington

Active

My name is Henry
I am seven years old
My favourite sport is football
I even play in the cold
I have a dog called Bella
She is a crazy little fella
I like to take her on a walk
Where she likes to play
Even though I don't like
To do it on a rainy day.

Henry Chapman (7)
Joydens Wood Junior School, Wilmington

Michael

M ichael is my name
I like playing the Minecraft game
C ats, dogs, animals I respect
H oneybees and wildlife I protect
A wesomely funny jokes I make
E verybody laughs their heads off
L ove making animal memes.

Michael Nikulin (8)
Joydens Wood Junior School, Wilmington

This Is Me

T iny in size
H appy always, but also sad
I am creative
S illy and funny at all times

I love my teachers
S peak a lot

M aths is my favourite subject
E aster is my favourite holiday.

Heashika Sivakumar (7)
Joydens Wood Junior School, Wilmington

This Is Me!

Always happy
I am always kind
And have a clever mind
Love to make friends
But some friends pretend
Love to draw
And love to explore
Always creative
And always competitive
At home I am silly
And super crazy
This is me.

Harshika Sivakumar (10)
Joydens Wood Junior School, Wilmington

Autistic Me

A lways repeating myself
U sually losing my temper
T oo much energy
I nterrupting people when they are talking
S creaming about midges
M ishearing and sometimes don't hear anything.

Rio Merja (8)
Joydens Wood Junior School, Wilmington

How To Make Me

Ingredients:

A pinch of mischief
A heaped tablespoon of cool
A little bit of spy
A shake of good running
A dash of drumming
A sprinkle of rainbow
50g of good gaming

First, add a small pinch of mischief (but not too much)
Next, you need a heaped tablespoon of coolness
Then you must not forget a little bit of spy
Before adding in a good shake of running
After, mix in a dash of drumming skills
Following this, an important step, is to add a sprinkle of rainbow
Last but not least, add 50g of absolutely amazing gaming
After 60 minutes of baking
I will most certainly be ready
And you will definitely enjoy!

Prince Gachogu (10)
Oasis Academy Watermead, Sheffield

This Is Me

T aking care of others is something I like to do
H onesty I embody, this is true
I love to do incredible writing
S uper artwork of mine is quite the sighting

I nteresting facts are always on my mind
S o other people know I'm kind

M um named me Billie, that's who I am
E veryone knows me and they're a fan!

Billie Machin (11)
Oasis Academy Watermead, Sheffield

This Is Me!

T his is me, Yara,
H onesty is what I do, that's true.
I love fluffy, puffy cats... *meow!*
S o I am also generous and calm.

I nteresting artefacts amaze me,
S itting by the sunset is my favourite thing.

M cDonald's is delicious
E meralds are like diamonds, that's me.

Yara Tahir (11)
Oasis Academy Watermead, Sheffield

David, That's Me

It's me, I'm back
My name is David
And I have a cat
He is called Neo
And wow he is fat
Because he ate all of the rats
I like KFC but ! must stay healthy
Then I get to see the great DC
After all of that, I will sleep
At night-time, I will count sheep
In the morning, going to school
I'm really cool
I'm David M and...
This is me!

David Moraru (10)
Oasis Academy Watermead, Sheffield

This Is Me

This is me, I like to sleep
I like going to Poundland because it's cheap
My favourite history topic is Greek
My favourite movie is DC
Then I go to sleep
My favourite animal is a sheep
My favourite car is a Jeep
Then I go back to sleep.

Mohammed Tarram (11)
Oasis Academy Watermead, Sheffield

Who Am I?

I am knocking on your door
Saying, "Take a treat!"
I am getting lots of candy
And some 50ps.

Coming down the chimney
My elf will see you
Next to the Christmas tree
I will see you next year
Don't shed a tear.

Shannelle Kelly (10)
Oasis Academy Watermead, Sheffield

Me And Danny

I am the fastest person
I am a lightning bolt

I am a dog lover
I am a cat hater

I will teach people football
I am the kindest person

I am helpful
I am courageous

I am funny
And my friend, Danny, is too

He is kind
I am kind
We are all kind

I am messy
I am fun
I make people laugh

I am a small size
I love to learn

This is me.

Evie-Grace Bailey (7)
Peel Park Primary School, Accrington

How To Create Me

To create me, you will need:
A teddy filled bedroom
A sprinkle of shyness
A dash of happiness
A teaspoon of friendliness

Now you need to:
Get a teaspoon of friendliness
And mix in a sprinkle of shyness
After that, stir in another teaspoon of friendliness
And a dash of happiness
Finally, get the teddy filled bedroom
And put it in the fridge to set.

Charli Molloy (7)
Peel Park Primary School, Accrington

This Is Me!

I am a spider lover
I am a cat cuddler
I love chicken nuggets
My eyes are coloured hazel
My size is small but my heart is big
I love all my friends and my friends love me
We all love each other
My favourite colour is pink
I love my mum and dad, my sister and brother too
I love all my family, no matter what
This is me!

Paige Carlton (8)
Peel Park Primary School, Accrington

This Is Me

T iny in size
H ave an amazing maths brain
I love Match Attax
S ometimes, I have a movie night

I love sports day
S ometimes I go over to my friend's house

M cDonald's is my favourite place
E very day I go for a walk.

Amir Mufleh (7)
Peel Park Primary School, Accrington

I Am Special

I am special
I love my mummy
Because she looks after me

I am special
I am frightened of spiders

I am special
I like to jump on the trampoline
With my sister

I am special
Because I am helpful to everyone.

Melissa Courtney (7)
Peel Park Primary School, Accrington

This Is Me

I am as funny as a comedian
As fast as a cheetah
I love pizza

I am very sporty
Faster than Usain Bolt

Sometimes, I spray paint my hair
With a little help
Because everybody
Needs a bit of help

This is me.

Ruby Pilkington (8)
Peel Park Primary School, Accrington

Me And My Friend

I am sporty
She is fast

I am good at goalkeeping
She is a good striker

I love apples
She likes strawberries

We're both fast

I am kind
She is lazy

This is me.

Danny Walker (7)
Peel Park Primary School, Accrington

I Am Special

I am special
My mum takes care of me

I am special
My mum helps me with my homework

I am special
My nana cleans up every day

I am special
I like going to the shop with my mum.

Jordan McCormack (8)
Peel Park Primary School, Accrington

This Is Me

I am kind
I am playful
I am as fast as a car
I am as funny as a chameleon
I am as smart as can be
I am frightened of rats
But I love unicorns
My eyes are like the blue sky
This is me.

Mia Johnstone (7)
Peel Park Primary School, Accrington

This Is Me

I am funny
I am really fast
I love my birthday
I love Christmas
I am seven years old
I am a dog kisser and cuddler
I like McDonald's and KFC
I like basketball.

Summer Crabtree (7)
Peel Park Primary School, Accrington

Me

I am...
A horse lover
Spider hater

Dad and Mum lover
Winter hater

Summer lover
Cold weather hater

And finally...
I am a good kid.

Shanum Zaheer (7)
Peel Park Primary School, Accrington

This Is Us

You like football
I like dancing

You like burgers
I like doughnuts

You like cars
But I like cute bunnies

Together we both like Pop Its.

Erin Daniels (7)
Peel Park Primary School, Accrington

I Like, I Like

I like my mummy
I like my daddy
I like to run like a cheetah
I am as cheeky as a monkey
I like running even though I am cheeky
I have a loving heart.

Tyler Gibson (7)
Peel Park Primary School, Accrington

This Is How I Think I Am

I like playing
I like playing football and reading
I like playing games
I love my mum and I like doing sport
I hate spiders
I like basketball.

Ramzaan Ali (7)
Peel Park Primary School, Accrington

This Is Us

I like dancing
You like singing

I like ice cream
You like doughnuts

Me and you like chocolate
Together we have a big heart.

Sophia Hosker (7)
Peel Park Primary School, Accrington

This Is Me!

Ginger, perfect the way I am
Be afraid, I have a plan
Artistic, brave, that's what they say
I have a plan to run away

Ready for take-off, that's what they say
Into the future, that's what they say
Creative with a great mindset
This year will be the best

Fast, but not that quick
It seems time has caught up
But it is not over yet
The future will come

Getting home is easy for me
Back in time, I'm coming home
Back at home at last
This year has gone so fast

Mathematics is my key
Hopefully not my only

It seems that my time is up
I have enjoyed makings words work

Jolly, happy, that's who I am
I am the secret man...

Ryan Moore (10)
Singlewell Primary School, Gravesend

This Is Me!

I am quiet
I am as shy as a little girl
I am magnificent, majestic me
I am bold
I am brave
I am awesome, amazing me
I am a cat lover
I am a student from Singlewell
I am not a person who is always with a tool
I am me, that's who I am
If I was an animal, I would be a pigeon
No one would bother me
I could stay in a tree
It might be odd, but it is me
If I was a food, I would be a cabbage
No one would eat me that much
I would roll my way through life
It is odd, well I don't care
Because I am me
And no one can change me!

Anya Ceka (8)
Singlewell Primary School, Gravesend

This Is Me

I am brave when I face fears
I am strong when I exercise
I am honest when there's lying
I am caring for others
I am respectful to others
I am peaceful to other people in a fight
I am happy every time
I am cool with everyone
I am kind when new people come
I am helpful when others need help
I am gentle when others are hurt
I am loving to everyone, no matter what
I am good at football against my friend
I am nice when I make friends.

Yannis Kamdem (9)
Singlewell Primary School, Gravesend

This Is Me

My name is Henry
Exploring is my thing
Never give up on my dream
Refreshing holidays with my team
I will never quit because my dream will come true
Sharing and caring is my thing
Hungry snacks just for me and my friends
Navigating treasure with my dog
Landing on islands that never end
Eating and drinking to be hydrated
You have no idea how long I've waited to tell you my story
Let it shine with all its glory.

Henry Shanley (7)
Singlewell Primary School, Gravesend

This Is Me

I have curly hair
So twirly and whirly
I like fidgets
And they're not like widgets
My friend is Tami
And she is happy
My friend is Mia
And she follows the trend
I like rock climbing
It's kind of like hiking
My name is Anayah
But my dad's higher
I don't like fire
I care for people
And my features are rare
I am unique and fair.

Anayah Chakravorty (8)
Singlewell Primary School, Gravesend

All About Me

I am a water guzzler
I am a book reader
I am a graceful ballet dancer
I am as kind as a nurse
My eyes are as blue as the sky
I am a bed snuggler
I am a fish when I swim
My hair is as yellow as the sun
I am a toast eater
I am a pet lover
Especially my cat, Molly
I love my family
Especially when I give my mummy a cuddle.

Emily Bishop (6)
Singlewell Primary School, Gravesend

This Is Me

What do I do?
I feel so clueless inside
My hands are trembling
Like a volcano erupting
I just want to hide!

Butterflies are swarming around
What if I'm found?
My hands are soaked in sweat
The shining sun is right beside me

They're watching me
But soon they'll see...
The true me.

Naveah Henry (10)
Singlewell Primary School, Gravesend

All About Me

I can howl like a wolf
I can do backflips like a kangaroo
I can snort like a pig
I am as fast as a cheetah
I am an animal lover
I am an expert drawer
I am as funny as a clown
My hair is as brown as chocolate
I am a great gamer
I am a kind brother
I am as cheeky as a monkey.

Judah Mangundu (6)
Singlewell Primary School, Gravesend

Albie

- **A** lbie is my name
- **L** iking pets is what I do best
- **B** ig, small, it doesn't matter, catching fish is what matters
- **I** n my house, I have got four pets
- **E** ating pepperoni pizza is what I do, it is lovely and scrumptious.

Albie Turner (7)
Singlewell Primary School, Gravesend

Joseph

J umping on a trampoline all the time
O bviously I like slime
S tanding on the line in goal
E ating all the chicken nuggets from my bowl
P laying with my friends
H oping my birthday never ends.

Joseph Brussee (8)
Singlewell Primary School, Gravesend

Fireworks

I can see red and pink fireworks and purple and orange
I can hear bangs, popping and sizzling
I can feel shocked and happy
I can smell smoke and fire
I can taste hot dogs and ice cream and hot chocolate.

Hollie Smith (6)
Singlewell Primary School, Gravesend

This Is Me!

I am as strong as a snake
I am as old as an old lady
I am like a magical wizard
I am as golden as the sun
I am as kind as a vet
I am as silly as a banana
I am like a party in the house
Who am I?

Sienna Roberts (7)
Singlewell Primary School, Gravesend

Who Am I?
A kennings poem

Fantasy footballer
TTRS champion
Raging runner
Glorious gamer
Tricky trickster
Dynamic football fan
Despiting darter
Exotic explorer
Sporting sportsman
Maths master.

Joel Gyateng (9)
Singlewell Primary School, Gravesend

All About Me!

A shley is my name
S inging is not my game
H aving fun in the sun
L azing about on my bum
E very day, eat a meal
Y ummy! Yummy in my tummy.

Ashley Payne (7)
Singlewell Primary School, Gravesend

Who Am I?
A kennings poem

Great gamer
Amazing actor
Disney lover
Chocolate eater
Tremendous dodgeballer
Warm hugger
Halloween adorer
Trick or treater
Curious watcher
Happy flower.

Olive Owen-Harvey (9)
Singlewell Primary School, Gravesend

This Is Me

R eading is my favourite thing to do
H orrid Henry is my favourite show
Y azoo milkshakes are my favourite thing to drink
S paghetti is what I like to eat.

Rhys Hutchinson (7)
Singlewell Primary School, Gravesend

This Is Me!

I am as caring as a dog
I am as kind as an ambulance
I am as funny as a YouTuber
I am a superstar criminal
I am a little lonely
I am a popular pufferfish
Who am I?

Aston Moody-Gbasai (6)
Singlewell Primary School, Gravesend

Who Am I?
A kennings poem

I am a...
Fast runner
Number cruncher
Brave footballer
Funny friend
Animal lover
Malteser muncher
Brilliant baker
Fun footballer
Silly swordfish.

Cameron Bennett (9)
Singlewell Primary School, Gravesend

Who Am I?

A kennings poem

I am a...
Gymnastics lover
Small daydreamer
Cheeky chatter
Mischievous muncher
Pizza eater
Dog adorer
Animal lover
Brave bender
Sporty runner.

Ella Parkinson (9)
Singlewell Primary School, Gravesend

When Autumn Falls

I see broken prickly leaves
I hear wind and rain
I smell spaghetti
I taste gingerbread men
I feel a warm campfire.

Alba Young (4)
Singlewell Primary School, Gravesend

When Autumn Falls

I see leaves falling
I hear leaves crunching
I smell chicken curry
I taste tomato soup
I feel wet trees.

Elsie Olatoye (5)
Singlewell Primary School, Gravesend

When Autumn Falls

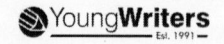

I see leaves falling down
I hear crunchy leaves
I smell bonfires
I taste hot chocolate
I feel cold.

Max Cavey (4)
Singlewell Primary School, Gravesend

When Autumn Falls

I see leaves falling
I hear raindrops
I smell soup
I taste gingerbread men
I feel wet.

Finley Mepstead (4)
Singlewell Primary School, Gravesend

Fireworks

I can see fireworks
I can hear bangs
I can smell burning
I can feel squishy marshmallows.

Cerys Jarvis (5)
Singlewell Primary School, Gravesend

Fireworks

I can see fireworks
I can hear fireworks
I can smell smoke.

Milana Bomiriyage (5)
Singlewell Primary School, Gravesend

This Is Me, Daksha

A caring mother bird
Making sure her eggs are safe from harm
Being aware every second that she has to be with them
That is how caring I am

I am precise like my dad
When he is working away
Listening and speaking
With a serious expression

I am independent like a cat
Who is playing with a ball of yarn by itself
Being happy and content and feeling confident
With how its life is

I am as calm as the silver shining moon
Shining down on the people
Making sure people are cool and relaxed

I am as energetic as a kid
Who had a candy overflow

And who is now running around
In circles all night

I am as determined as an eagle
Attempting to grab its prey
So its family won't go hungry

I am humorous like a comedian
Who is making people burst out in laughter
And getting hiccups
I am brave like a soldier in the army
Sacrificing their life for their country

I have jet-black hair
As straight as a tree
With bangs moving side to side

I have dark brown eyes
As dark as chocolate
From Sainsbury's

I love family like a baby does
When they are born needing care

I love reading
Like a squirrel loves its nuts
Gathering and munching on them

I love travelling around the world
Eating different cuisines
Jumping into different oceans and pools
Sipping a tropical drink
While hiking in the dense rainforest
Listening to the chirping of birds

I do not like hatred or discrimination
Because of anything that makes someone different

This is Daksha Mishra
This is who I am
As my personality and appearance
My likes and dislikes
This is me!

Daksha Mishra (9)
Southbank International School Kensington, Notting Hill

I Am Frida

I am calm like a warm breeze
Bright like a peaceful, smooth sea
As relaxed as a joyful sapphire wave

I am creative, crafty
Like a musical painting

Tortoise lover
Chocolate demolisher
Amusing books reader

Dark chocolate amber eyes
Almond brown hair

As balanced as someone
Who eats candy and healthy food
As caring as a cosy fire
Warming up on a winter's day
As mindful as a peaceful, warm sleep

You do you and that is true!

Frida Gauder (9)
Southbank International School Kensington, Notting Hill

This Is Me, Mason

I am curious like an investigator
Figuring out the mystery

I am an entertaining joke-teller
Making family laugh
I am funny like a comedian

I am helpful
Friendly
Helping people when people are depressed

I am almost the tallest
Towering over my friends

School is exuberant
Learning
Playing

Dumplings are fantastic
Soft on the outside
Juicy with pork

Surfing is the best
Riding on the wave feels like I'm gliding

Chicken is awful
Texture, fatty strands

Going upstairs is a bummer
Hard work
Huff puff!

Steak is gross
Pink blood dripping inside

I am fast like a race car
But not coming in first place

Cycling to Borough market
With my mum

My name is Mason
And I like making cakes.

Mason Sheckman (10)
Southbank International School Kensington, Notting Hill

This Is Me!

I'm like a wolf
Exploring places

If something dangerous
Is about to happen
I'm always up to challenge

If my pack is hurt
I am quick-witted
And know exactly what to do

I'll always be brave
To help someone or myself

When my pack and I find a home
With my creativity
Everything quickly turns fascinating

My chestnut fluffy fur
Is unique to the pack
My chocolate eyes
Shimmer in the sun

But the bad weather comes
Millions of droplets shower down

When the day is almost done
Playing video games
Is the thing I like to do

Along with watching anime
And YouTube
With this, I drink some bubble tea

But smoke rises up
Cigarettes are scattered
All over the floor

I clean them up
The radiant sun shines softly.

Luisa Nutz Wloch (9)
Southbank International School Kensington, Notting Hill

This Is Me, Sadie

I am fearless
I am like a cheetah
Sprinting through the foggy forest
Ready to pounce at my greatest fear

I am fearless
Even if my team is down
I still stand persistent
Like an emperor penguin
Ready to take on anything

I am fearless
I am like a Chinese dragon
With colours that glisten
In the sunlight
It has no wings
Though it still flys high

I am fearless
My pack is frail
Like a sloth
Still I make them
Chuckle and grin

My sapphire eyes narrow to the prey
Light rain trickles down my face
I know I am small
But I'm still fierce

And that's all I need to know.

Sadie Tomlin (10)
Southbank International School Kensington, Notting Hill

This Is Me!

I'm brave like a lion
Fighting its prey
As it runs fast

I am creative
Like an artist
Thinking about
Bright colours
In my inspiring mind

I am caring to my family
And friends as they need help
Around the world

I can be nimble
As I play football
With my bright sapphire eyes

Crowd encouraging me
To think like a winning player

My amber hair falls down
My back as I read a joyful book

I loathe apples
Sticky sweet watermelon
As I sit in the sunshine
By the glistening ocean
Makes me happy

I can make people chuckle
Hilarious jokes
Energetic.

Ella Piro (10)
Southbank International School Kensington, Notting Hill

Chance The Great

I am calm
Like the waves
In the ocean breeze

I am wise
Like a 239-year-old owl
Who has read
All the books
In the Oxford library

My hair is as fluffy
As a cloud
Floating in the sky

Spiders freak me out
Like a cat being chased
Through water
By a dog

I am energetic
A kid who ate
Way too much
Luscious candy

Celery is absolutely, horridly
Disgustingly stringy

Christmas is
Magically joyful.

Chance Coughlin
Southbank International School Kensington, Notting Hill

This Is Me!

I'm Imogen
When I'm older, I want to be a horse rider
and horse jumper
Not a horse racer
I'm older than the old days
I'm taller than I was when I younger
I didn't ride when I was ten and under but
now I can
I like dogs, animals, horses and also my friend
from school
Also, when I'm older, I want to own a farm
With rabbits, dogs guinea pigs and horses
With excellent horse riders, trainers and farmers
I want people under twelve to do horse riding
lessons at the farm
I love my family, I have two sisters
I have two dogs, I have a pug and a pug-cooper-
staffy
I also have a hamster called Basil
He is blonde and very fluffy and cuddly
That is my life and what I hope happens.

Imogen King (10)
St Anne's CE Primary School, Oldland Common

What Makes Me Me

I am an animal lover, it's my dream to be a vet
Even though I have some information, I'm not quite ready yet
Especially for spiders, creepy crawlies give me the creeps
When I'm around complete strangers I cower like a sheep
My love of most animals grows day by day
But I'm not fond of cats, I'm sorry to say
Some words to describe me are chatty, confident and loving
Although I love animals, there's another little something
Another of my strong points is that I'm an excellent fighter
When I'm sparring, my rage and anger flares up like a candle lighter
I have many qualities that you may not be able to see
But they are all that makes me me!

Amelia Woodland (10)
St Anne's CE Primary School, Oldland Common

This Is Me And My Football

I am the Flash in my football boots
As a defender so good, I send a shiver down your spine
My one and only weakness is the ball itself
Getting hit in the face is my one weakness, so I stay clear
I must follow the ball and deny my fear
My fear is just a little bubble
The ball comes towards me and I never know what to do
But it's too late now, it is my cue
I've got the ball, dive left, do a one-two
It swoops and glides and guess what?
It goes in
After the match, celebrations arise
The next match awaits
Adrenaline and pride fills us up

Off we go again, will victory be ours?
We are not and never will be sore losers
Or sour winners, we are fair.

Alex Wood (10)
St Anne's CE Primary School, Oldland Common

This Is Me

I am a tree
Each leaf is a different side to me
My writing is the gold bit
Shining in all its glory
The falling brown leaves
The fear of anything gory
And when a blustering storm of a day comes
My branches hold me up
My wonderful family, who I love dearly
Red, scarlet leaves show my angry side
Whilst orange leaves show my stressed side
My brain's my bark
Blotting out horrible people
And my emerald, budding leaves
Are my developing talents
This beautiful multicoloured tree
In all its artistry
With all its diversity
And its different sides
All of it, in all its rainbow colours
All represent me!

James Rigby (10)
St Anne's CE Primary School, Oldland Common

This Is Me

My name is Brayden and this is my poem
I like the glamorous grass and the staggering trees
I love playing football outside and I support Bristol City
My favourite player is Andi Wiemann because I like the way he plays football
I have a dog called Stan, who is a border terrier that I love very much
I also have two siblings, a sister called Molly and a brother called Ryley
My parents are very kind and caring towards me and my siblings
In school, my favourite subject is science and my second favourite is maths
I hope that one day I can play for Bristol City and make me proud
I will never change who I am for anyone or anything.

Brayden Hembrough (10)
St Anne's CE Primary School, Oldland Common

Me!

I am a dedicated football fan
I always try to show up to training and matches when I can
I am as quick as a flash with a ball to my feet
Sometimes, when I come out of a challenge
I end up with only one cleat
I am always confident to go in for a tackle
Don't try and win yourselves or you'll be in a battle
But when I hop on my mountain bike, I'm always ready for a send
I absolutely love going on bike rides, even on the weekend
When I'm riding along the cycle track with ease
I feel a strong, cold gust of the breeze.

Colby Walker (11)
St Anne's CE Primary School, Oldland Common

This Is Me

I'm Poppy and this is my poem
Here's some of my favourite people:
Peggy (my dog)
Ammo (my other dog)
Akina, Emily, Freya and my family
Here's some of my favourite belongings:
My book
My glasses
My phone
My favourite place is my living room
My favourite subject in school is science
Here's some of my friends:
Akina
Emily
Freya
I like me and I'm never going to change
For anyone or anything
I flow like a poppy, sting like a nettle.

Poppy Forbes (10)
St Anne's CE Primary School, Oldland Common

Dog

I have a dog called Remi
She is very stubborn
And very naughty

She nibbles my toes
But is very friendly
She is only playing
And is very shy
She hates walks
And is very lazy

Even though she is annoying
I still love her and I'm sure you will too
I will have her forever and never let her go
She has a very loud bark
That is how they speak
She will live until twelve
And then I will be twenty-two

This is me.

Danilo Amato (10)
St Anne's CE Primary School, Oldland Common

This Is Me!

I am a jigsaw of feelings and emotions
I am frightened of many things, although
Creepy crawlies and horrifying spiders are
one of my foes
Caves and tunnels make me feel trapped inside

Though I'm not always a scaredy-cat
And when the footballs are not flat
I shall run past the defence as quick as a flash
And the net behind the goalie will get a little bash

I am a jigsaw of feelings and emotions.

Mollie Bateman (11)
St Anne's CE Primary School, Oldland Common

This Is Me

There are many pieces to me
I am frightened of messing up a skill
Panicking makes me make a mistake
But when it comes to a competition, I go
I always turn up to lessons
I'm an annoying little sister
But caring and kind

My dog makes me feel joyful when I am down
My dog is always by my side
And it loves me
I'm a kind, brave, beloved girl
I also look up to people when they're down.

Katie Phillips (10)
St Anne's CE Primary School, Oldland Common

Mighty Me

M arvellous - I am gifted with talent and emotional strength to overcome whatever I face ahead

E quality - I am equal to my friends and family who make me laugh heavily and I like how they help me in life.

We can learn that we are unique
And we were born for a purpose
Everyone is equal
And we should make sure
We aren't being mean to certain people
We should remember
We are all the same.

Temini Ezobi (11)
St Anne's CE Primary School, Oldland Common

This Is Me

I am like a puzzle
Some pieces are hard to find
It's the height of tall buildings
That sends shivers down my spine
When the adrenaline builds up
I feel like I'm coming to an end
But when I get on my mountain bike
I will prepare myself for a send
Even on a long hike,
Usually on the weekend
I wouldn't care about the destination
Because all that matters is the elation.

Andrew Tresise (11)
St Anne's CE Primary School, Oldland Common

This Is Me

My dream when I'm older
Is to be a famous wakeboarder
And to have a farm and a horse
I'm older
You're younger
I'm shorter
You're taller
We are different
And nothing can change that
If you want to do dance, you do that
Nobody can make you change your mind
Do what makes you happy
And do what makes you you
That is what I think
And it works.

Lily-Mai Williams (11)
St Anne's CE Primary School, Oldland Common

This Is Me!

There are many sides to me
I am an amazing rugby player and horse rider
But when it comes to creepy crawlies
Arachnophobia is my fear
Shelob the spider, she takes over me
Like a volcano ready to erupt

I am a strong girl, I am not afraid to tackle
When I mount into the saddle
My day becomes better by the minute
I am brave
I am strong
I am funny
This is me!

Summer Currey (10)
St Anne's CE Primary School, Oldland Common

This Is Me!

There are many pieces to me
I am frightened of messing up
I am scared of meeting new people
But I enjoy sports
It makes me smile
When I am alone
And have no one to talk to
I listen to music

My cat makes me feel joyful
When I am down
My cat is always by my side
And it loves me
I'm kind and helpful
And I look up to a lot of people.

Tom Gregory Fear (10)
St Anne's CE Primary School, Oldland Common

Achieve Your Dreams

I am unique
You are unique
We are unique
Everybody is different
I like kickboxing
You like rugby
Nobody is the same
No one in this world is the same
Everybody is different
The whole world will never be the same
No one will set foot on this earth
With the same body as you
You can do anything
As long as you set your mind to it.

Amela Levett (10)
St Anne's CE Primary School, Oldland Common

This Is Me!

I am a very kind person
But I am nervous around big crowds
When I'm at home
My cat and bunny comfort me
Roller skating is my dream and nightmare
When I'm on my skates at home, I feel free
But when I am on the road
I am scared I will scratch my knee
When I am around strangers
I am worried that if I talk too much
I may be in danger.

Myla Bliss (10)
St Anne's CE Primary School, Oldland Common

This Is Me!

I am full of skills and talent
As soon as I hit the saddle
As soon as a crop lands in my hand
My confidence grows bigger and bigger

When cantering at one with my pony
I think of nothing but how happy I am
After dismounting, I pick out his hooves
Groom him
Then let him out in the yard

I am brave
I am courageous
I am me!

Lotti Butler (10)
St Anne's CE Primary School, Oldland Common

We Are Different!

I am different
You are different
We are different
Nobody is the same
Especially you
Down to the food we like
Or the dreams we dream
I want to be a vet
While my friend wants to be a teacher
I like netball
While my friend likes dance
Nobody who ever set foot
On our planet is the same
And that's just the way I like it.

Alana Spiller (10)
St Anne's CE Primary School, Oldland Common

Love Is True

My life is full of love
That comes from above
I wore my love like a glove
I wear it all the time
When I'm ready to shine

As I laugh
My neck pulls my chin up
Like a giraffe
When I smile
I'm there for a while
And when I'm sad
My family feels bad
But other than that, love is true
When I'm with you.

Ava Humphries (11)
St Anne's CE Primary School, Oldland Common

The Dream!

I am dreaming
I am dreaming
Of a land of peace
A land of love
A land of fortune
Where the impossible is possible
Where life is calm
Where harmony holds strong
A place where the sun shines
A place where water glitters
Somewhere to love
To worship
To be you
This is what I dream!

Lauren Smith (10)
St Anne's CE Primary School, Oldland Common

This Is Me

This is me that no one could be
I love food and I don't have a mood
I'm very happy and dotty
And I love me
I care about family
And I love my granny
I love to eat and listen to a beat
I love me
And everybody
Do you like to drink?
If so, I'll give you a wink
And that's me.

Noah S (10)
St Anne's CE Primary School, Oldland Common

You Can Do Anything As Long As You Set Your Mind To It

This is for faith
This is for belief
This is for peace
I like to dance
You like football
Nobody is the same
And will never be
You do things to be happy
I do things for peace
And harmony
The world could never be the same
You are unique
And believe in the person you are.

Maisie Townsend (10)
St Anne's CE Primary School, Oldland Common

Dreams

Although this fellow may be scared
He faces challenges to be dared

He may not be good all the time
But he always tried to strive

This boy never rests
Because he dreams to be the best

Some things he won't achieve
But he wants to reach his dreams.

Oliver Savage (10)
St Anne's CE Primary School, Oldland Common

Me!

I am funny
I am brave
I am kind
I am all of those beautiful things
This is me!

I like horses
I like family
I like food
I like everything
This is me!

Sometimes I cry
Sometimes I laugh
Sometimes I have the best time
This is me!

Brooke Lamb-Collins (10)
St Anne's CE Primary School, Oldland Common

Mighty Me

My name is Ben
I am unique
Because I'm always at my peak
I like hide-and-seek
I love science
I love maths
Never give up
You always have luck
Don't turn your back
On what you have
Always be kind
Therefore, you will find
A way to succeed.

Ben Kuciak (11)
St Anne's CE Primary School, Oldland Common

This Is Me!

When I'm older
I want to work in a jewellery shop
I'm older
You're younger
I'm taller
You're shorter
I have brown hair
You have blonde hair
We are both different in every way
No one can stop me being me.

Priya Ludwell (10)
St Anne's CE Primary School, Oldland Common

Me

I have many sides to me
I used to be scared of the sea
I get stressed
But no one is the best
When I'm at cheer
I feel like I have two homes
I even have flexible bones
I love my dog
He would jump into a bog
This is me.

Elise Bishop (10)
St Anne's CE Primary School, Oldland Common

This Is Me!

Dancing is my passion
It's what represents me
When I'm dancing
I feel as if I'm whisked away and free
My dream is to dance
In point shoes, so elegant to me
And when my dream comes true
I'll be elegant to you.

Amelia Stokes (10)
St Anne's CE Primary School, Oldland Common

This Is Me

On the court I'm an ace,
I'm a lightning bolt on the court,
The only deuce on the court is the juice I drink,
The net is my friend,
The lines treat me like a king,
The green turns to red so it's always in.

Daniel Darby (10)
St Anne's CE Primary School, Oldland Common

All About Me!

I am an animal lover
Tree climber
Nature explorer
Fast runner

My favourite animals are
Dogs
Cats
And tortoises

I'm a daredevil
I like scooters and skateboarding.

Ruby Bristow (11)
St Anne's CE Primary School, Oldland Common

This Is Me

T his is me
H umorous
I am Abi
S hining like a star

I am unique
S unny disposition

M agnificent
E pic.

Abi Lowman (10)
St Anne's CE Primary School, Oldland Common

This Is Me!

A kennings poem

There are many sides to me

Lazy boy
Pet lover
Smoothie slurper
Sweet gobbler
Fast runner
Football fan
Gaming master
Good sportsman
Goal saver.

Harvey Drew (10)
St Anne's CE Primary School, Oldland Common

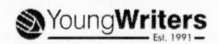

This Is Me!

When I'm older
I want to be a vet
I'm different
You're different
I'm taller
You're smaller
But we both care
And no one can change who I am.

Freya Kelly (10)
St Anne's CE Primary School, Oldland Common

This Is Me

This is me
I'm what no else one can be
I care about every animal and tree
I show kindness to everybody
I try to do everything respectfully
That's me.

George Hillier (10)
St Anne's CE Primary School, Oldland Common

This Is Me

It's strange you know but this is me
It's only the outside you're able to see
Inside of me where you can really dig deep
My thoughts, dreams and feelings are best when I'm asleep
Being only ten years old, I love all types of sport
But I've discovered basketball's a no-go because I'm kinda short
I use my voice for lots of things, especially when I sing
Let's hope I'm a pop star in the making
Who knows what my future will bring?
My next big adventure is moving to secondary school
I feel a bit nervous but I know it will be cool
Chatting with my friends helps me get things off my chest
Trust me, when you pick the right ones, they truly are the best

I'm up for a challenge and like to be pushed
But sometimes in life, your feelings can seem crushed
So be happy, spread joy and be as kind as you can be.

Darci Yates-Henry (10)
St Anthony's Catholic Primary School, Kingshurst

Birthdays!

B irthdays are the best!
I n birthdays you get to eat cake!
R eal birthdays mean fabulous presents.
T he best person in the world is erm... me!
H aving a great day if your birthday is on the 3rd of September.
D ecorations are amazing especially when they are full of sparkle and glitter!
A wesome, it's me here, my birthday!
Y ay! My favourite time of the year is here!

Ana Sandhu (8)
St Anthony's Catholic Primary School, Kingshurst

All About Me

L ovely to everyone
O utstanding creative writer
I ce cool, even when it is scorching hot outside
S illy Sausage.. sometimes

W inx Club is the best series
I love Christmas, winter is the best season
L icking ice cream tastes
S crumptious
O ranges taste juicy, they're great
N obody likes gummy bears.

Lois Wilson (7)
St Anthony's Catholic Primary School, Kingshurst

This Is Me

R ed roses are pretty and smell so sweet
O ptimistic that I will become a teacher and get to teach
S inging is my favourite thing to do
I nteresting like a maths lesson; times tables are tricky, it's true!
E ating yummy chicken nuggets and chips with red sauce, I love to do!

Rosie Brannigan (7)
St Anthony's Catholic Primary School, Kingshurst

I'm The...

I'm the...
I'm the joker king
I'm the basketball player
I'm the best Minecraft player of all time
I'm the best at timetables... test me
I'm a superstar at maths... try me
I'm an avid watcher of all that is YouTube
I'm me!

Bobbie O'Mara (8)
St Anthony's Catholic Primary School, Kingshurst

Things About Julia

J ust being funny, that's me
U rbanska is my last name
L ia is my most favourite name
I will be an Olympian star
A mazing, outstanding and beautiful... obviously me!

Julia Urbanska (8)
St Anthony's Catholic Primary School, Kingshurst

The Halloween Boogie

The night was black and the pumpkins glowed
There was no rain and it had not snowed
The ghosts were getting ready, to scare once more
The vampires were thirsty, you could hear the werewolves roar

The children were all dressed up to trick or treat
They danced down the street to the spooky beat
Skeletons danced and their bones would tumble
They feasted on candy and a giant apple crumble

It was all hallows eve and the party had started
The zombies were late and Frankenstein farted
They danced and they sang late into the night
The witches cast a spell and gave everyone a fright

Halloween was a blast and they wished it would last
They had the best time ever but it just goes too fast.

Elliott Marsden (9)
St Edward's Royal Free Ecumenical Middle School, Windsor

A Young Girl

One day a baby girl is born,
When she can walk, she hops around in the spring,
Admiring baby chicks and saplings like a baby fawn,
She sings merrily in the warm sun and plays on swings, having lots of fun,

In the summer she is taken to the shimmering blue sea,
Where she goes paddling and swimming,
Running around on the sandy beach, feeling free,
She collects smooth seashells and carefully climbs the slimy, jagged rocks,
Whilst wearing her favourite pink Crocs,
Her mother buys her a Mr Whippy even though her father reminds her it is a bit nippy,

As nature changes its season, the not so little girl learns about Guy Fawkes' treason,
In her gorgeous green wellies she crunches through the orange and golden leaves and begins to put up cobwebs and wreaths,
It's Halloween evening and everyone is going to have a startling fright,

It's a fearful night and there's only the glimmering moon for light tonight,
When all the goodie wrappers are dumped on the floor, our sugar-addicted girl wants more,

It's festive time, the time when you sing songs that rhyme,
Our Big Girl races excitedly outside to play in the snow, sporting a green and red hat tied with a bow, whilst thinking about the man of the month and his catchphrase "Ho, ho, ho."
The next day she hurriedly wakes up to find that Santa Claus has eaten all and drunk from the reindeer patterned cup,
She finds herself opening all her neatly wrapped parcels, receiving messages from old grannies and young aunties sending things like hand-knitted sweaters and fairy castles,
She makes her way over to the holly spring table where she wolfs down things like bacon but gives some to her puppy Mabel,
Later on, they head out for their traditional stroll and the girl's father picks up some extra coal,
Then they have a wonderful Christmas feast with all the trimmings, followed by fluffy, moist cakes, chocolate-coated puddings,

Our young girl lies in bed that evening full and well, wondering about her future and where she may one day dwell.

Elena Littlewood (11)
St Edward's Royal Free Ecumenical Middle School, Windsor

All About Me!

Me?
I've got a lot to say but hey let's talk about my day
I wake up in the morning with a smile on my face
I run downstairs to find my puppy in her special place
We have a lot of fun having breakfast on the run
Sometimes I have toast but I love waffles the most
My sister waffles such a lot
But I'm not going to waste my time
Even if it fits the rhyme!
Finally, it's the end of the day
But hey
I'm going home
I'll get my phone
And groan and moan
Till homework's done with help from Mum.

Liliana Baxendale (10)
St Edward's Royal Free Ecumenical Middle School, Windsor

Friendship Bee

Something was hovering in the sun
The sound it made, made all the children run
It looked like it was having fun
Look closer, it's not fun!
Now it wants to make me run

The colour of it is like honey
Surprise! It's a bumblebee
With her wings as good as gold
Friendly and loyal
It cheerfully hovered away...
Wait a minute...
I am the bumblebee!
Helpful and ready for more
Caring and sharing for all of you

No matter what life throws at us
We are all together
We are always going to be good friends
And today and the days after

Will be a new day to play
All together!

Bye-bye bumblebees.

Ayinoor Murray (9)
St Edward's Royal Free Ecumenical Middle School, Windsor

This Is Me

When I was one, I went on a twenty-six-mile run
When I was two, I invented a whole new type of shoe
When I was three, I climbed a tree with a girl called Lee
When I was four, I created a mechanical claw
When I was five, I performed for the Queen on YouTube live
When I was six, I made a house of cement and bricks
When I was seven, I got a reading age of 111
When I was eight, I got rid of all world hate
When I was nine, I mastered the art of swinging on a vine
When I was ten, I made the ultimate den, a pig pen!

Rose Jackson (10)
St Edward's Royal Free Ecumenical Middle School, Windsor

If I Were An Animal...

If I were an animal, I'd be a bear
Cute, cuddly and fluffy, all covered in hair

Sitting down and eating honey
Telling jokes, I am so funny

Helping my family
No one's looking uncannily

Out of home, I shall explore
The smell of roses I do adore

All my friends are so fun too
It's the trees we look through

Back inside, nice and warm
Always with my swarm

Dinner is always so nice
Summer pudding can be as cold as ice

Now it's time to settle down
Into bed, with the darkness all around.

Averil Newton (11)
St Edward's Royal Free Ecumenical Middle School, Windsor

This Is Me!

C ats are the number one best thing
H ilarious. Hilarious in one, hilarious in all
A mazing but fun, can't stop the fun
R ugby. Love the pitch, love the ball, can't stop playing till I fall
L ove. Love in the heart, warm and sweet, never too cold to say hello
O h, but too cool for school
T oo cool for school
T all, but cool
E nergy. Full of fun to bring back fun.

Charlotte Kieren (11)
St Edward's Royal Free Ecumenical Middle School, Windsor

My Dog

I have a dog named Wookie
She tries to eat my cookies
She tries to play with the ball
But then it bounces on the wall
I have to clean her when she is mucky
Which is not good because it is yucky
She is always eating things on the floor
Which is more annoying than ever before
But apart from that, she is the best dog ever
And I will always love her forever.

Willow Banasko-Lawson (10)
St Edward's Royal Free Ecumenical Middle School, Windsor

What Animal Am I?

My feet want to gallop
Every single day
I have a very long mane
And I eat hay
Sometimes I feel lonely
But that's okay
I'm very happy when my rider comes
To collect the often mail
My friends are white, brown and black
And I am grey
What am I?
I am a horse.

Chloe Balla (11)
St Edward's Royal Free Ecumenical Middle School, Windsor

This Is Me!

T all in height
H appy as can be
I like football
S wimming is what I'm good at

I love sweets
S ometimes I read books

M usic is my hobby
E xcellent at art.

Millie Mander (9)
St Edward's Royal Free Ecumenical Middle School, Windsor

This Is Me!

Out of all the children in my school
I may not be the tallest
All of the voices in the world
Mine may be the smallest
But I can almost touch the stars
If I stand on my toes
But when I say my words
I may change the world.

Maya Trevisan (9)
St Edward's Royal Free Ecumenical Middle School, Windsor

This Is Me

I am as silly as a goose
As crazy as a mad scientist
As happy as a dancing gorilla
As cheeky as a monkey
As loving as a happy panda eating its favourite bamboo
And as innocent as a crocodile
As bold as a lion hunting for its prey
As friendly as a swan.
This is... me!

Minahil Waqas
Thames Primary Academy, Blackpool

This Is Me

Let's add a teaspoonful of skiddishness
And a pinch of tiredness in the considerate bowl
Plus a batch of cuckooness
Then, a handful of thoughtfulness
In the oven after it's hardened
Add some clumsy icing
Then lots of odd sprinkles.

Thomas Hill (10)
Thames Primary Academy, Blackpool

This Is Me

I like to act and that's a fact
I like to sing, my dog has one wing
I am very quirky
I love Christmas turkey
I am really crazy
I do know someone called Maize
I am extremely silly
I don't like chilli con Carne
This is me!

Florence Brown
Thames Primary Academy, Blackpool

Me

I am as beautiful as the sun
I am as clumsy as can be
I am as happy as a girl going home after school
I am as sleepy as a little baby
I love travelling in the spot of light
I am always kind and never stop smiling
This is me!

Najwa Raisa
Thames Primary Academy, Blackpool

This Is Me!

A giant droplet of cheekiness
And a teaspoon of extraordinary
A whole lot of love
Mix until creamy and fluffy
And add the main ingredient…
A ginormous splodge of bonkers!

Lexi Glover (9)
Thames Primary Academy, Blackpool

This Is Me!

I am as happy as the sun
As silly as fun
As royal as a queen
As scary as the sea

I enjoy to wander
I am a scientist
I like to think
And problem solve

This is me!

Hallie Taylor
Thames Primary Academy, Blackpool

This Is Me

I'm a crazy, lazy boy
I'm a sleepy, weepy boy
I'm a yawning, spawning boy
I'm a gamer, tamer boy
I'm a happy, snappy boy

This is me...

Gabriel Bennett (9)
Thames Primary Academy, Blackpool

Young Writers
Est. 1991

YOUNG WRITERS INFORMATION

We hope you have enjoyed reading this book – and that you will continue to in the coming years.

If you're the parent or family member of an enthusiastic poet or story writer, do visit our website www.youngwriters.co.uk/subscribe and sign up to receive news, competitions, writing challenges and tips, activities and much, much more! There's lots to keep budding writers motivated!

If you would like to order further copies of this book, or any of our other titles, then please give us a call or order via your online account.

Young Writers
Remus House
Coltsfoot Drive
Peterborough
PE2 9BF
(01733) 890066
info@youngwriters.co.uk

Join in the conversation!
Tips, news, giveaways and much more!

YoungWritersUK YoungWritersCW youngwriterscw